CRYPTOCURRENCY GLOSSARY AND
BITCOIN
COLORING BOOK

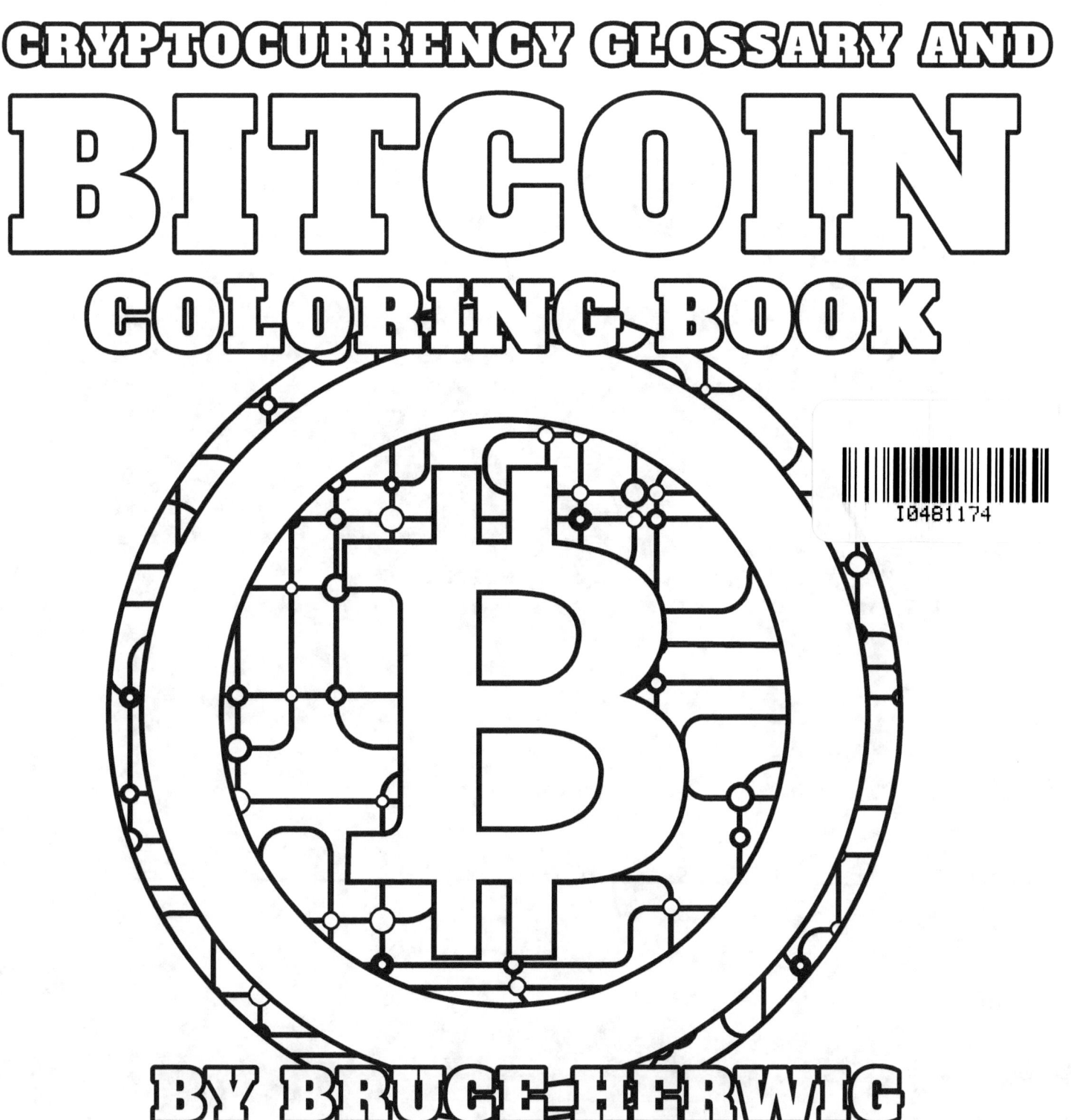

BY BRUCE HERWIG

Coloring book art by Redlands, CA artist Bruce Herwig
Follow this link for some FREE bonus coloring pages:
www.bruceherwig.wordpress.com/Bitcoin

Feel free to copy these pages for your personal or classroom use.
Please encourage your friends to get their own copy.

☀ Color At Your Own Risk ☀
Side effects include stress relief, mental clarity, smiles and fun!

I0481174

A BLOTTER PAGE IS RECOMMENDED IF YOU ARE COLORING WITH MAGIC MARKERS.

A blotter page is a sheet of paper you place under the page you are coloring to absorb the magic marker that will sometimes bleed through on to the page below.

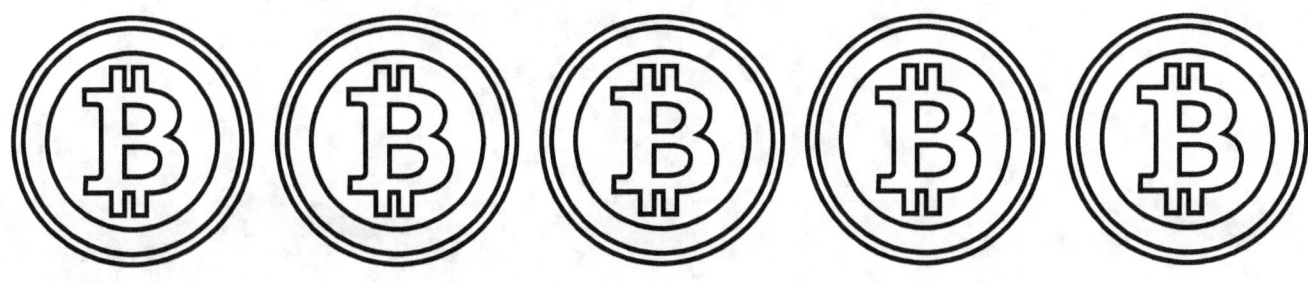

WHAT IS BITCOIN?

Bitcoin is a type of digital currency in which encryption techniques are used to regulate the generation of units of currency and verify the transfer of funds, operating independently of a central bank.

ALTCOIN

An altcoin is the community accepted name for any coin that isn't Bitcoin. A form of cryptocurrency that has the same decentralized, peer-to-peer principles as bitcoin, but which uses its own blockchain and has its own rules of operation.

BLOCK

Blocks are found in the Bitcoin block chain. Blocks connect all transactions together. Transactions are combined into single blocks and are verified every ten minutes through mining. Each subsequent block strengthens the verification of the previous blocks, making it impossible to double spend bitcoin transactions.

BIP

Bitcoin Improvement Proposal or BIP, is a technical design document providing information to the bitcoin community, or describing a new feature for bitcoin or its processes or environment which affect the Bitcoin protocol. New features, suggestions, and design changes to the protocol should be submitted as a BIP. The BIP author is responsible for building consensus within the community and documenting dissenting opinions.

BLOCK CHAIN

The Bitcoin block chain is a public record of all Bitcoin transactions. You might also hear the term used as a "public ledger." The block chain shows every single record of bitcoin transactions in order, dating back to the very first one. The entire block chain can be downloaded and openly reviewed by anyone, or you can use a block explorer to review the block chain online.

BLOCK HEIGHT
The block height is just the number of blocks connected together in the block chain. Height 0 for example refers to the very first block, called the "genesis block."

BLOCK REWARD

When a block is successfully mined on the bitcoin network, there is a block reward that helps incentivize miners to secure the network. The block reward is part of a "coinbase" transaction which may also include transaction fees. The block rewards halves roughly every four years.

CHANGE

Let's say you are spending $1.90 in your local supermarket, and you give the cashier $2.00. You will get back .10 cents in change. The same logic applies to bitcoin transactions. Bitcoin transactions are made up of inputs and outputs. When you send bitcoins, you can only send them in a whole "output." The change is then sent back to the sender.

COLD STORAGE

The term cold storage is a general term for different ways of securing your bitcoins offline (disconnected from the internet). This would be the opposite of a hot wallet or hosted wallet, which is connected to the web for day-to-day transactions. The purpose of using cold storage is to minimize the chances of your bitcoins being stolen from a malicious hacker and is commonly used for larger sums of bitcoins.

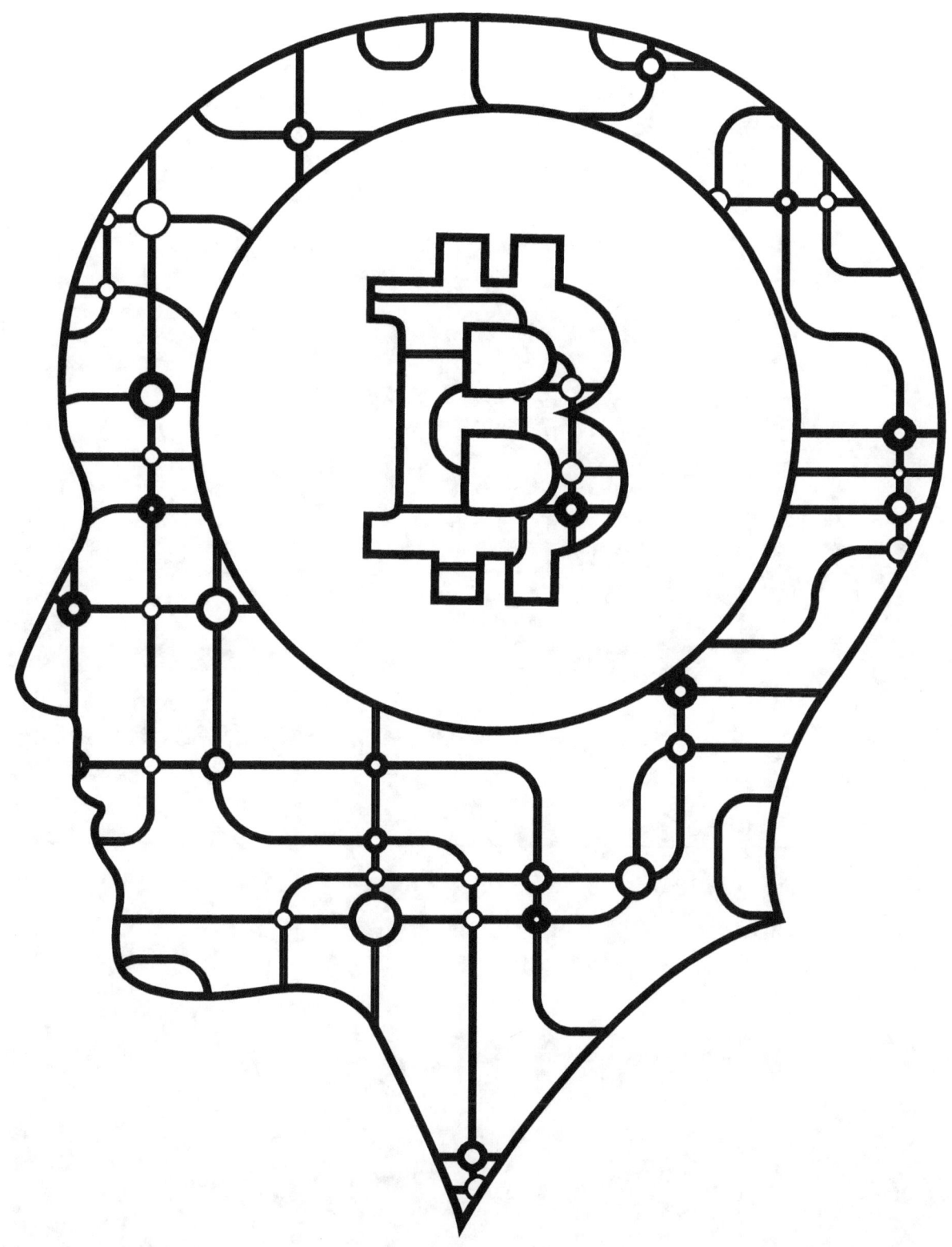

CONFIRMATION

A confirmation means that the bitcoin transaction has been verified by the network, through the process known as mining. Once a transaction is confirmed, it cannot be reversed or double spent. Transactions are included in blocks.

CRYPTOGRAPHY

Cryptography is used in multiple places to provide security for the Bitcoin network. Cryptography, which is essentially mathematical and computer science algorithms used to encrypt and decrypt information, is used in bitcoin addresses, hash functions, and the block chain.

DECENTRALIZED

Having a decentralized bitcoin network is a critical aspect. The network is "decentralized," meaning that it's void of a centralized company or entity that governs the network. Bitcoin is a peer-to-peer protocol, where all users within the network work and communicate directly with each other, instead of having their funds handled by a middleman, such as a bank or credit card company.

DIFFICULTY

Difficulty is directly related to Bitcoin mining (see mining below), and how hard it is to verify blocks in the Bitcoin network. Bitcoin adjusts the mining difficulty of verifying blocks every 2016 blocks. Difficulty is automatically adjusted to keep block verification times at ten minutes.

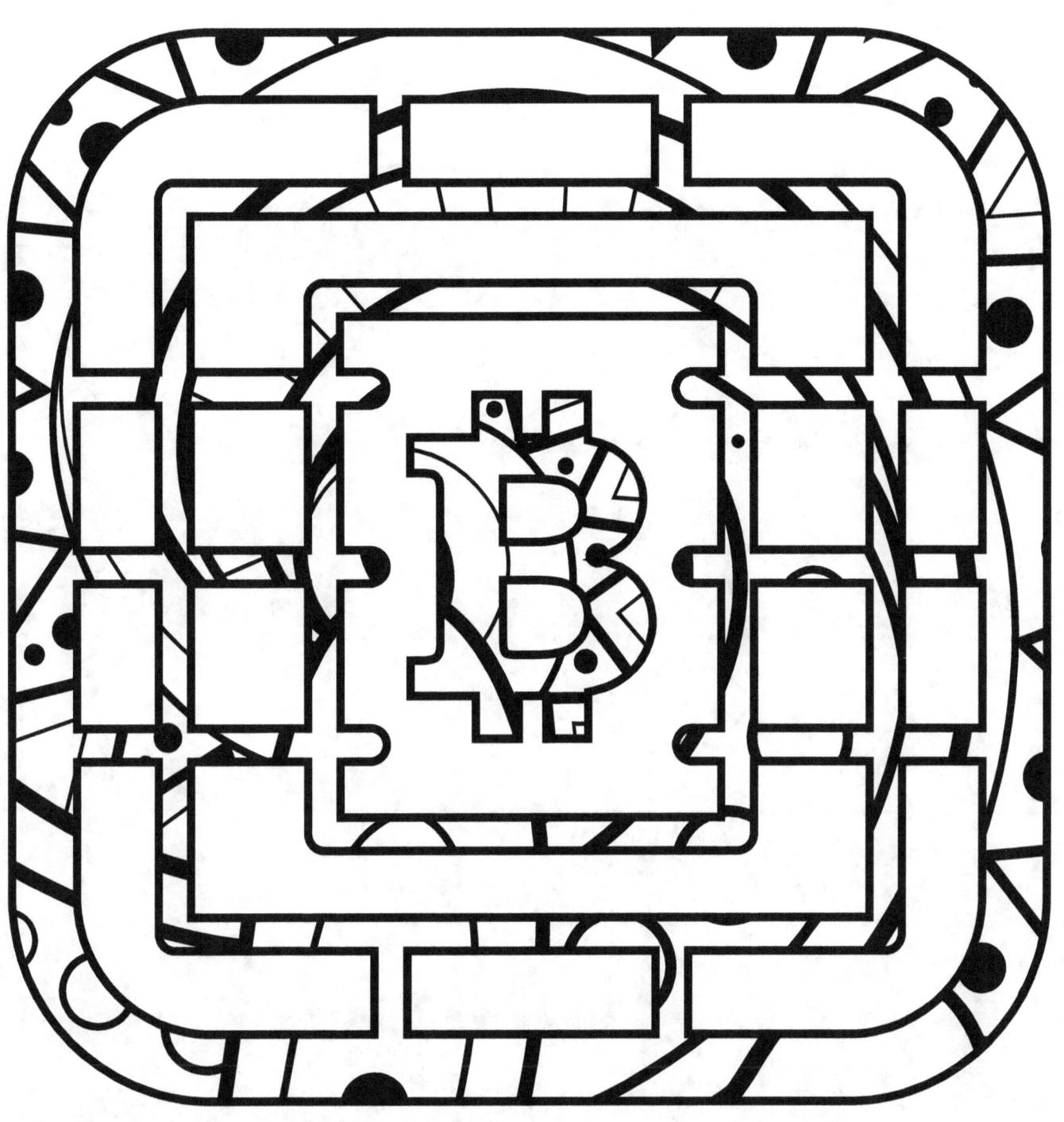

DOUBLE SPEND

If someone tries to send a bitcoin transaction to two different recipients at the same time, this is double spending. Once a bitcoin transaction is confirmed, it makes it nearly impossible to double spend it. The more confirmations that a transaction has, the harder it is to double spend the bitcoins.

FULL NODE

A full node is when you download the entire block chain using a bitcoin client, and you relay, validate, and secure the data within the block chain. The data is bitcoin transactions and blocks, which is validated across the entire network of users.

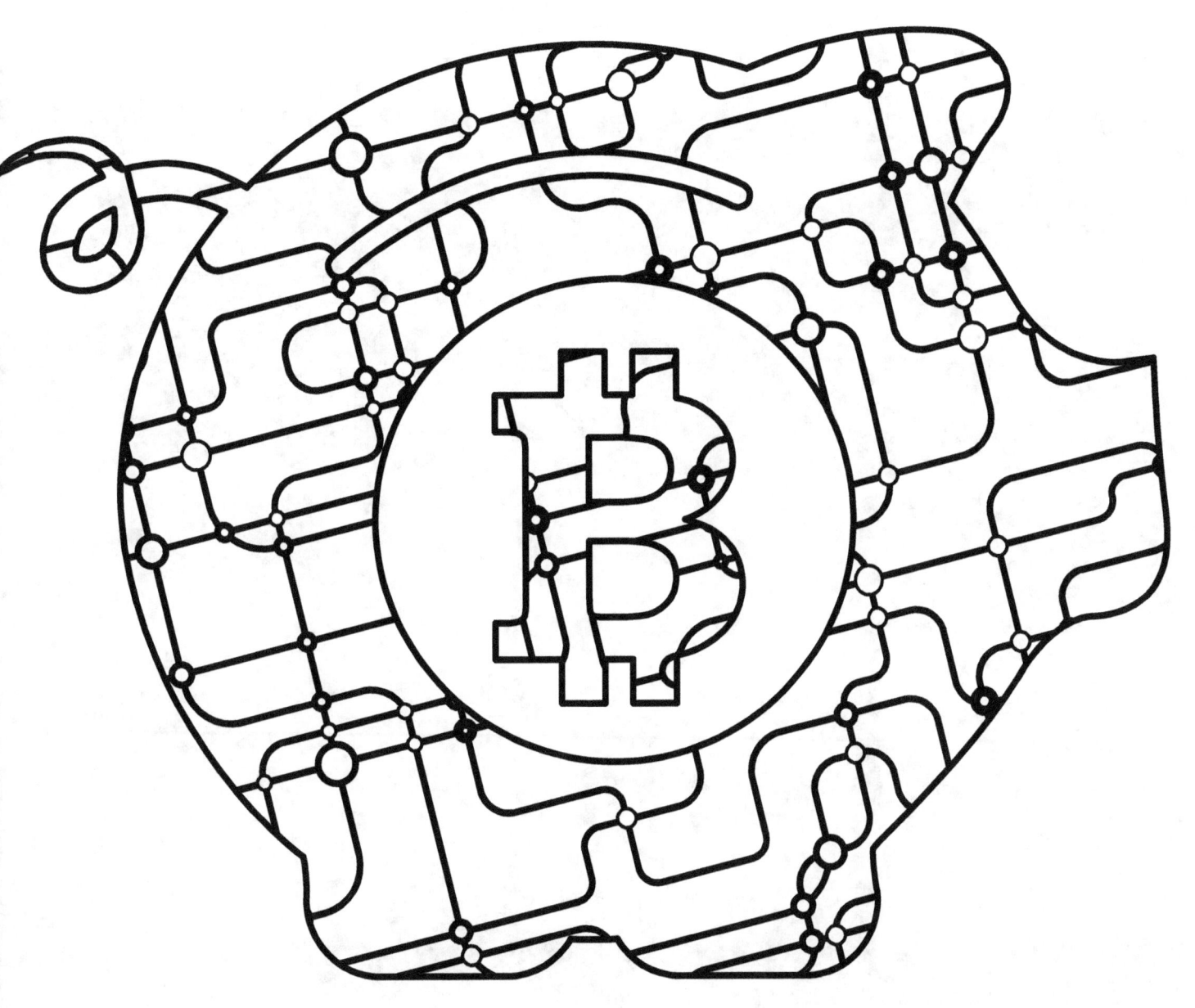

HALVING

Bitcoins have a finite supply, which makes them scarce. The total amount that will ever be issued is 21 million. The number of bitcoins generated per block is decreased 50% every four years. This is called "halving." The final halving will take place in the year 2140.

HASH RATE

The hash rate is how the Bitcoin mining network processing power is measured. In order for miners to confirm transactions and secure the block chain, the hardware they use must perform intensive computational operations which is output in hashes per second.

MINING

Bitcoin mining is the process of using computer hardware to do mathematical calculations for the Bitcoin network in order to confirm transactions. Miners collect transaction fees for the transactions they confirm and are awarded bitcoins for each block they verify.

PEER-TO-PEER

Peer-to-peer (P to P) computing or networking is a distributed application architecture that partitions tasks or workloads between peers. Peers are equally privileged, equipotent participants in the application. They are said to form a peer-to-peer network of nodes.

POOL

As part of bitcoin mining, mining "pools" are a network of miners that work together to mine a block, then split the block reward among the pool miners. Mining pools are a good way for miners to combine their resources to increase the probability of mining a block, and also contribute to the overall health and decentralization of the bitcoin network.

PRIVATE KEY

A private key is a string of data that shows you have access to bitcoins in a specific wallet. Think of a private key like a password; private keys must never be revealed to anyone but you, as they allow you to spend the bitcoins from your bitcoin wallet through a cryptographic signature.

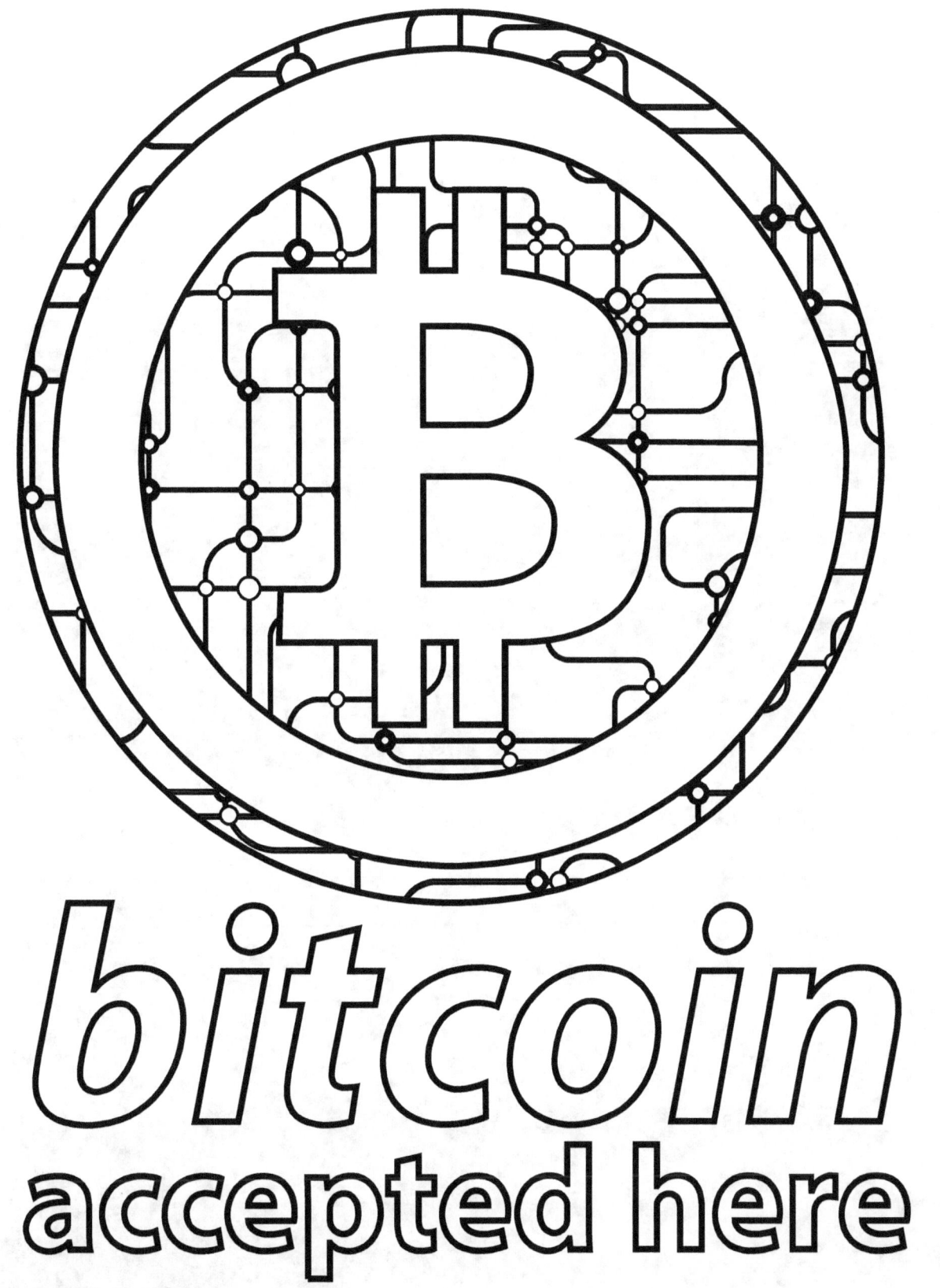

PROOF OF WORK

Proof of work refers to the hash of a block header (blocks of bitcoin transactions). A block is considered valid only if its hash is lower than the current target. Each block refers to a previous block adding to previous proofs of work, which forms a chain of blocks, known as a block chain. Once a chain is formed, it confirms all previous Bitcoin transactions and secures the network.

PUBLIC ADDRESS

A public bitcoin address is cryptographic hash of a public key. A public address typically starts with the number "1." Think of a public address like an email address. It can be published anywhere and bitcoins can be sent to it, just like an email can be sent to an email address.

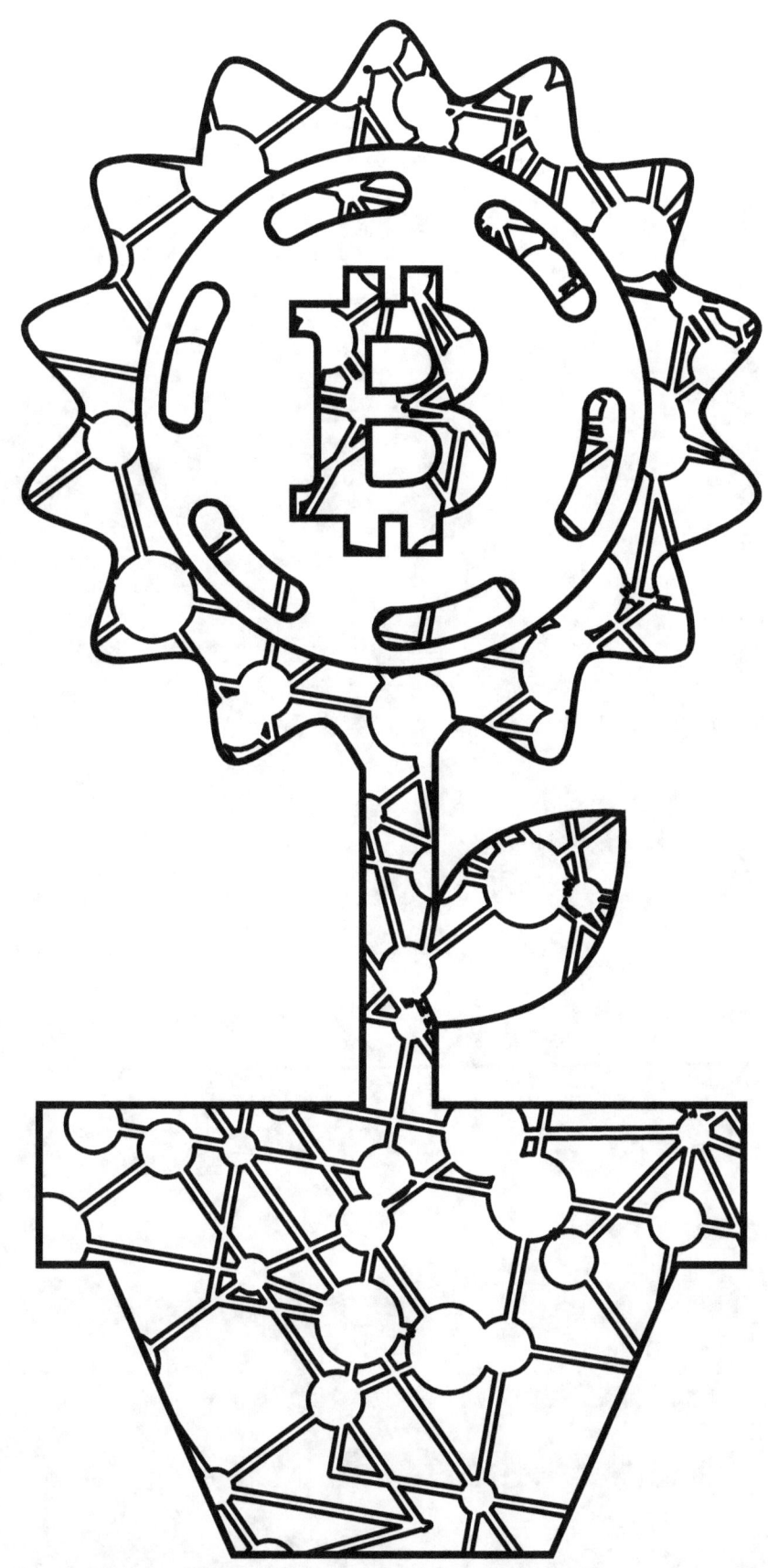

SATOSHI NAKAMOTO

Bitcoin's existence began with an academic paper written in 2008 by a developer under the name of Satoshi Nakamoto. Satoshi is the name used as the original inventor of Bitcoin.

SATOSHI

The smallest divisible unit of one bitcoin. There are 100 million satoshis (8 decimal places) in one bitcoin. One satoshi = 0.0000001 bitcoins.

TRANSACTION

A transaction is when data is sent to and from one bitcoin address to another. Just like financial transactions where you send money from one person to another, in bitcoin you do the same thing by sending data (bitcoins) to each other. Bitcoins have value because it's based on the properties of mathematics, rather than relying on physical properties (like gold and silver) or trust in central authorities, like fiat currencies.

TRANSACTION FEE

All cryptocurrency transactions involve a small transaction fee. These transaction fees add up to account for the block reward that a miner receives when he successfully processes a block.

VOLITILITY
It is a rate at which the price of a investment increases or decreases for a given set of returns. Volatility is measured by calculating the standard deviation of the annualized movement over a given period of time.

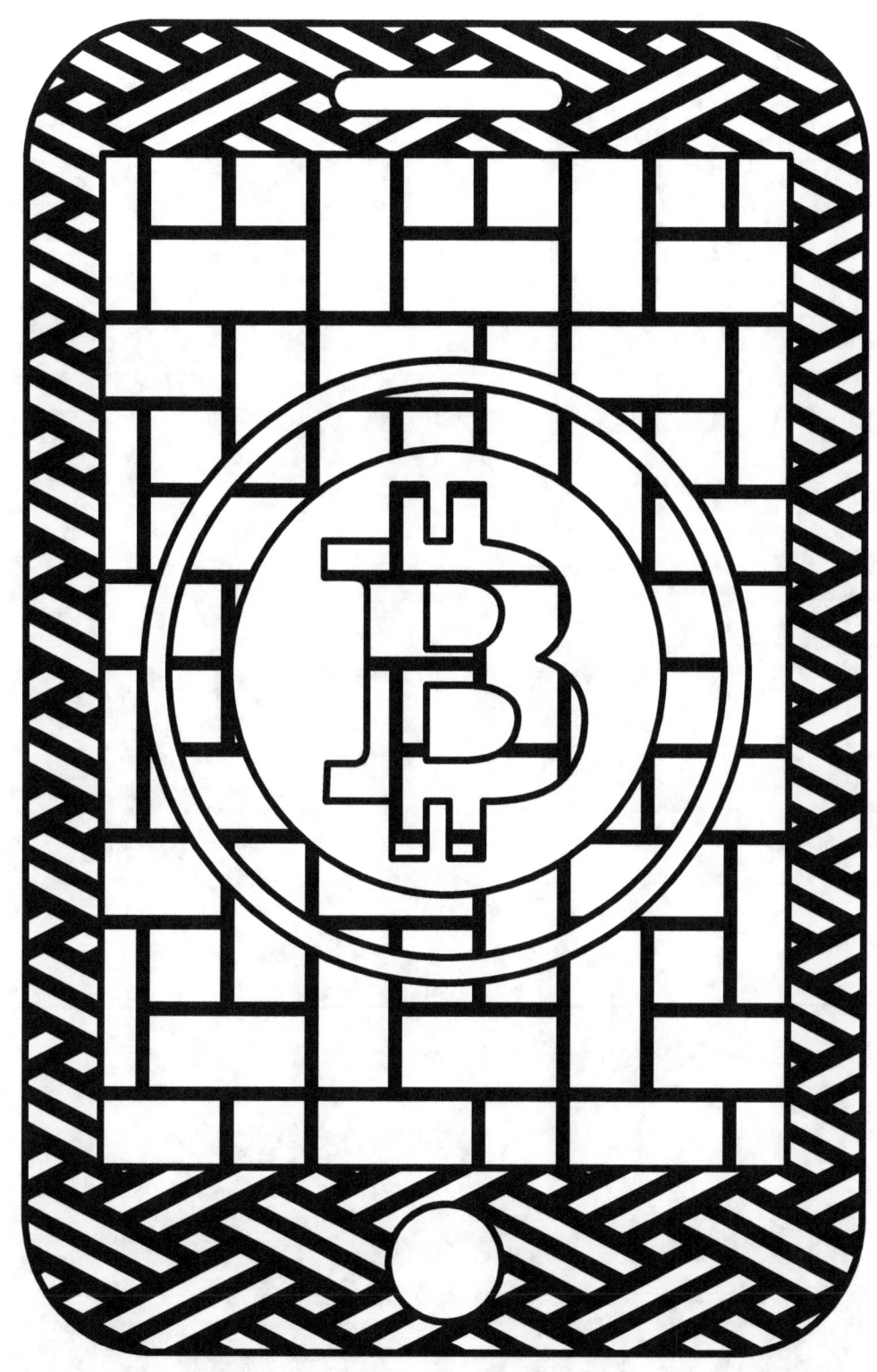

WALLET

Just like with paper dollars you hold in your physical wallet, a bitcoin wallet is a digital wallet where you can store, send, and receive bitcoins securely. There are many varieties of wallets available, whether you're looking for a web or mobile solution. Ideally, a bitcoin wallet will give you access to your public and private keys. This means that only you have rightful access to spend these bitcoins, whenever you choose to.

TEST PAGE

Use This Page To Test Out Color Combinations

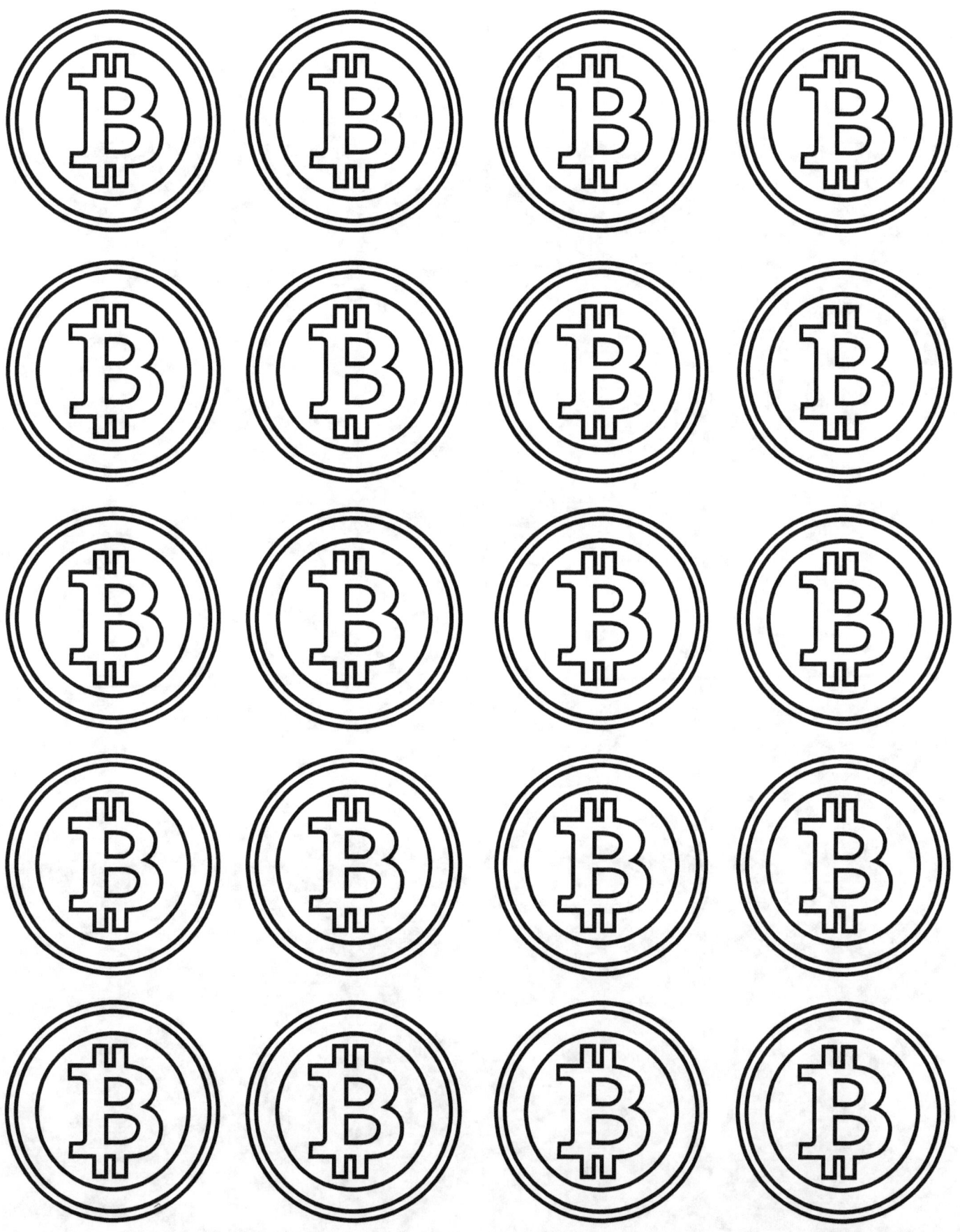

TEST PAGE
Use This Page To Test Out Color Combinations

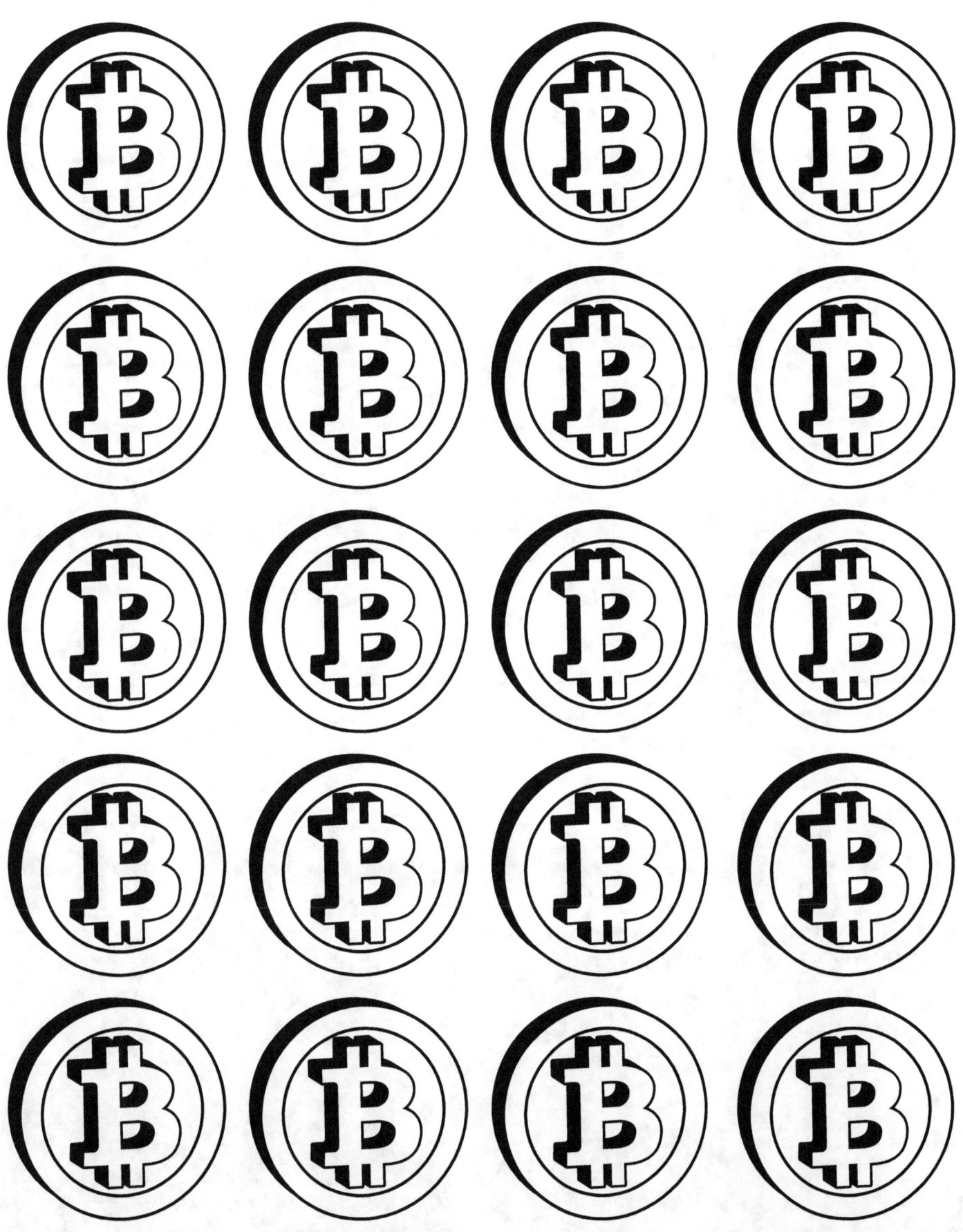

BONUS COLORING PAGES

NINJAS ATTACK!

NINJA ADVENTURE COLORING BOOK

www.bruceherwig.wordpress.com/NinjasAttack

YIN AND YANG

TORII GATE

If the Sky Could Dream...

Dragon Coloring Book

www.bruceherwig.wordpress.com/Dragons

HE HAD ONLY HEARD OF DRAGONS,
AND ALTHOUGH HE HAD NEVER SEEN
ONE, HE WAS SURE THEY EXISTED.

DEE MARIE - SONS OF AVALON: MERLIN'S PROPHECY

It is one thing to read about dragons and another to meet them.

URSULA K. LE GUIN, *A Wizard of Earthsea*

FIDGET SPINNER FUN!

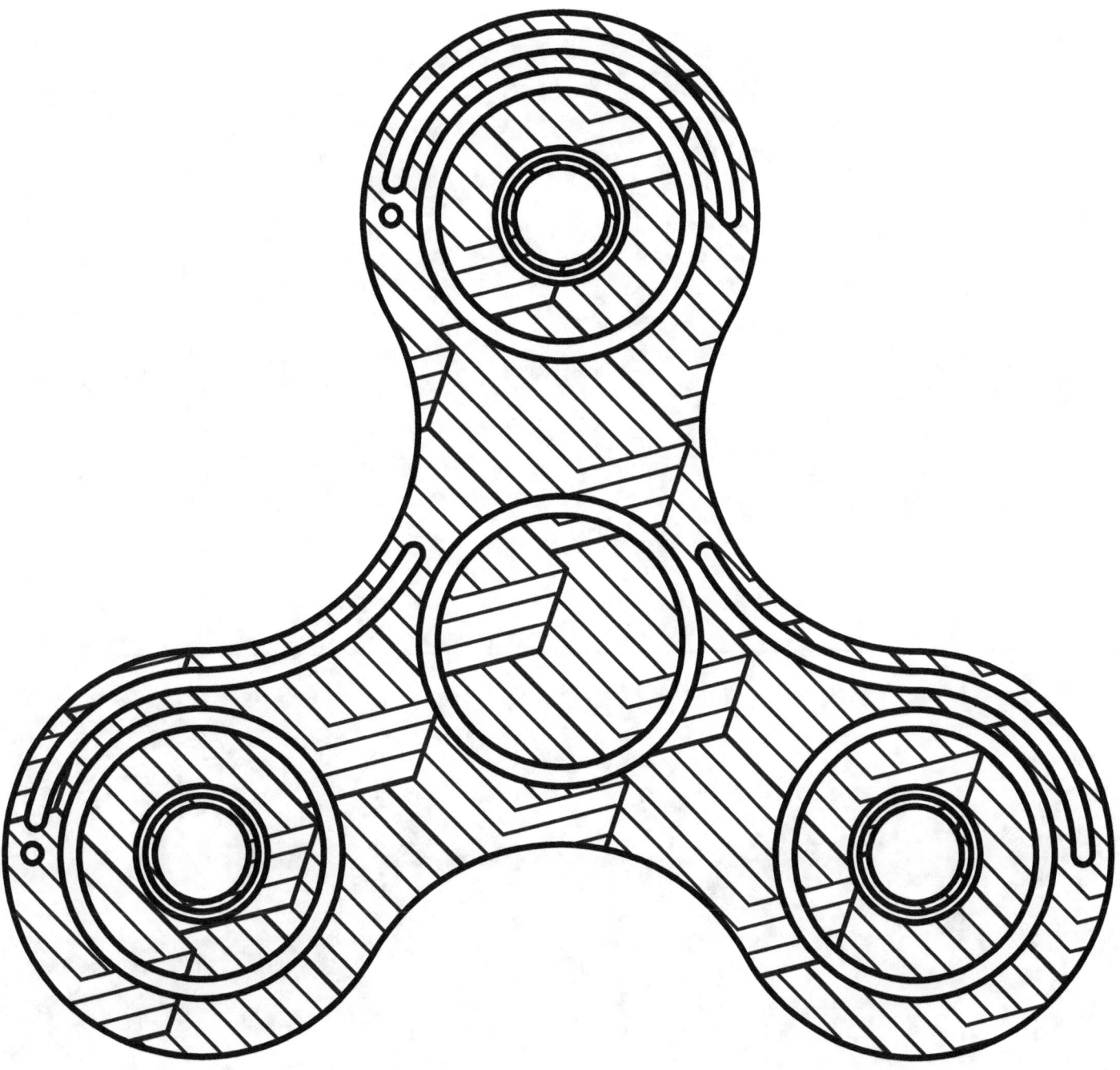

ACTIVITY COLORING BOOK

www.bruceherwig.wordpress.com/FidgetSpinner

SCAN TO WATCH A VIDEO

FIDGET SPINNER CHALLENGE
You can buy fidget spinners in all kinds of colors and designs.
They even have some that glow in the dark!

FIDGET SPINNER CHALLENGE

Can you pass a fidget spinner from one hand to the next while it is still spinning?

CRAZY CRITTERS
AMAZING ANIMALS A-Z
www.bruceherwig.wordpress.com/CrazyCritters

BUTTERFLY

ACKNOWLEDGMENTS

Several of the bitcoins icons were made by Freepik from www.flaticon.com. Additional images used from stock.adobe.com and vecteezy.com. Bitcoin terms and glossary were gathered from a variety of sites on the Internet, including blockgeeks.com, blockchain.com and wikipedia.org.

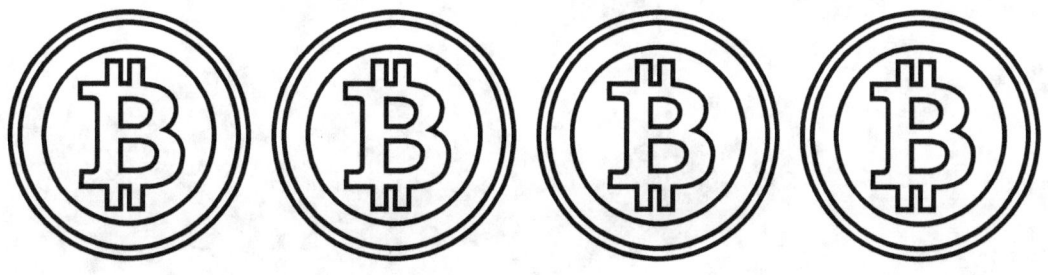

www.ingramcontent.com/pod-product-compliance
Lightning Source LLC
Chambersburg PA
CBHW081740220526
45468CB00008B/2181